Why Fashion Matters: One Woman's Theory of Retail

Lynn Ujvary

With Katy Ujvary

Lynn Ujvary can be contacted at lynn@swishladieswear.com

Photography by: Ted Peters

Published by Prominence Publishing
www.prominencepublishing.com

ISBN: 978-1-988925-13-4

Dedication

Thanks mom and dad for believing... some sooner, some later.

Table of Contents

What is SWISH?

We are SWISH. Maybe you know us, maybe you don't. We're happy to meet you. Welcome! Take a load off, grab a cup of tea. Put your feet up. This is going to be fun, we promise.

SWISH, as a concept, has existed in the heart of Lynn Ujvary (founder, owner, designer and confidence inspiration extraordinaire) for much longer than we've been a public entity. When she was growing up, her family didn't have a lot of money. Twice a year, the kids were taken on a grand adventure to the plush carpets and fancy salon of the department stores, and a new outfit was selected, carefully. Trying on the many options, and putting on a show for their hard-working parents, the ultimate approval would hopefully escape her mother's lips. "That's SWISH." And that's when you knew it was really special.

Then they would head home, and with whatever her mum approved of and purchased, they would have a fashion show for her dad, and anything he liked got labelled REALLY SWISH.

And that is what dressing should feel like every day. SWISH.

In a world where the fashion industry looks at themselves as the high authority of beauty, worthiness, and self-worth, we strive to show all women that they deserve to feel SWISH. To look in the mirror and gasp at how damn GOOD they look. To learn how to feel like that every day, and to make it easy and effortless.

Hey, we see you raising your eyebrows. It is possible. Yes, for you, too. Have you seen yourself, girl? You're a stunner! Don't worry, this is only page one. You'll get it before we're done.

Society has made fashion a bit of a war on women. Everywhere, we see magazine covers with models so photoshopped that even they don't look like that. We're told that as women, we need to age backwards, and be so thin that we disappear when we turn sideways. And, it's BULLSHIT. It's time to set the record straight.

At SWISH, we know that every woman is unique and special in her own way, and deserves to be honoured and celebrated every day of the year. It's not about size, it's not about colour, it's not even about fashion. It's about feeling good about yourself, and who you are. Right now.

Welcome to the revolution.

Chapter One: From Concept to Design

SWISH, as an enterprise, started as Lynn's hobby, to keep her sane while she worked at her "real" job. It began as an experiment, a theory about clothes and how women should dress, how they could dress. And so, with a degree in Fashion Design, and 30 years of experience in retail and customer service, SWISH was born.

Using her technical knowledge, and the wisdom she had gained as a woman who had dressed herself since she was old enough to know it was too cold for shorts in February, Lynn was ready to put her theory to the test. She scoured the market looking for clothes that would help her illustrate her philosophy, basically, how to use clothes to make the most of our assets, highlight everything we love about ourselves, and focus on building confidence. She was sorely disappointed by how slim the pickings were.

Not to be outdone by such a simple setback, Lynn pulled out her pencil and ruler, and set about correcting the issue. Armed with her own designs, and a mind full of endless possibilities, it was time to change perspectives through engineered design.

What is engineered design? Don't worry, it sounds more complicated than it is. Magic? Sometimes, but not so scary. Engineered design is the ability to manipulate clothing so that you can highlight and flatter, or camouflage and deflect. And, the advantage of designing with your hands, a pencil, ruler, and a warm body, is that all the styles that are created this way are tried and true. No science experiments concocted in a lab, or on a computer screen, somewhere. Just your body, and the fabric.

In all her years in the fashion industry, Lynn knows that fundamentally, most women want to be 20 years younger and 20 pounds lighter. And, as the birthday candles multiply, the pressure and expectation to look the same as we did in our younger years builds.

And, we're not exempt when we're young either. Women in their 20's and 30's aren't 100% happy with their bodies either, there's always a little something that they wish was more/less. Rarely is there a woman in a changeroom who is thrilled to death with everything she puts on. But, that's where engineered design comes in. We focus on the parts that you are thrilled with and build confidence by accentuating those features, as well as pulling it all together with the right pieces and the right accessories. At the end of the day, it's not the clothes that make you glow. You're glowing because you feel confident, beautiful, and ready to take on the world.

Still confused? Let us tell you about this one time...

Liz came into the store and needed a dress for an upcoming wedding. Specifically, her husband's daughter's wedding. Not her step-daughter's wedding, her husband's daughter's. You don't have to work hard to see that she was nervous and it was pretty clear how she felt about her position in the family. After chatting with her a little more, it came out that this was going to be the first family function where everyone was going to be there – including the ex-wife – and she was TERRIFIED.

So, we asked her, "Do you want to stay in the shadows, escort your husband, and stay out of the way? Or, do you want to knock it out of the park?" Her face lit up, and she said, "Let's knock it out of the park!"

After a discussion about what she liked and didn't like, colours she preferred, what styles she normally wore, she and Lynn walked through the store together and picked out a few dresses. Liz tried on the dresses, but something wasn't quite... SWISH. Lynn took a quick tour of the store, and came back with an outfit she thought would compliment Liz's figure and colouring. In this case, a simple dress, and a tuxedo back blouse. It wasn't what she thought she was coming in to buy, but, the silhouette hit her perfectly, and the colours made her blue eyes pop! Liz was a sporty girl, and felt slightly out of place in a traditional dress, but that was what she thought she was expected to wear. When she was able to try an outfit that let her personality and confidence shine through, she was able to "knock it out of the park", while still looking 100% wedding appropriate.

A few weeks after the big day, Liz dropped into the store again. She came armed with photos, and, as a result of being able to be herself, relax, and feel confident in how she looked, she wound up having a great time at the wedding, even making friends with the rest of the family! And, as an added plus, she was looking forward to the next event, when everyone would gather at Christmas.

So, what does that mean for you? Confidence is contagious, my dear, and you're about to catch the bug! Have you ever had that outfit that was exactly right?

"I just feel GOOD in it." Well, heck, that's what we're going for here. What if every outfit in your closet made you just feel GOOD? What a concept.

So, reject the concept of "appropriate dress" (puke, am I right?), and let's get you in the show stoppers.

Clothing doesn't make the first impression, how you feel in the clothing makes the impression. Not to sound hokey, but confidence comes from within.

Chapter Two: Who's Who and How Trends are Made

F ashion trends. We read the magazines, we pore over trend reports to see if we'll be wearing pastels or jewel tones, florals or geometrics... Stripes, polka dots, or plaid?!

Honestly, the trend reporters are just marketing experts who give it their best guess... It's a little like playing the fashion stock market.

Of course, there are influences: TV, social media, celebrities, world events and leading designers (oh la la, did you see what Chanel had on the runway this season? Genius!).

But, we're going to let you in on a little secret (shhhhh.... Don't tell!). Do you know who actually sets the trends? You do. The shopper. The person who actually buys and wears the clothes.

Now, don't let it go to your head. But, when you think about it, it really makes a lot of sense. If manufacturers make wide leg jeans and no one buys them... Not really a trend, was it? And, they definitely won't be making them again next year.

On the other hand... If they make wide leg jeans, and they are the best thing that ever happened, and everyone loves them, manufacturers will make them season after season and a trend is born!

Chapter Three: Retail Culture/"The Industry"/Ethical Manufacturing

W hat is fast fashion? Fast fashion is just that – clothes produced fast, sold fast.

It's said that a fast fashion retailer can take a style from runway, make a pattern, sample, produce and have it stores worldwide in two weeks.

These factories are usually in 3rd world countries, poor conditions, long days and weeks for poor pay. The quality is sometimes compromised for low retail costs, so more western consumers will buy them, wear the clothing a few times, throw it out and then go shopping again. The shopping cycle starts again and more shopping equals more profit.

What is slow fashion?

Slow fashion in our modern culture is the classics. Clothes that bridge trends and are relevant over many years. They are made with quality fabrics and manufactured to last. At SWISH, we define slow fashion a little differently.

Slow fashion is where last year's clothing classics work with this year's prints and colours. We want to update what's in your closet so our new styles build on what you already have. We think this is how it should be done!

What is Ethical Manufacturing?

We all love a good deal. Five dollar t-shirts are hard to pass up. But, the thing that you have to remember is who had to make sacrifices for that good deal. How do you pay for the fabric, the sewing, the shipping... the list goes on, and sell it for $5.00. Doesn't make it such a good deal anymore, does it?

At SWISH, we practice Ethical Manufacturing. This means a fair day's work, for fair pay, healthy working conditions, and reasonable hours. All our clothes are manufactured in Vancouver, at a factory that pays a living wage and works within the labour laws laid out for people working in Canada. This means we can monitor the conditions of the factory, meet and get to know the people whose hands have made our clothes, and know that they are well taken care of, and happy.

We see our designs through from start to finish, and we know who worked on every step. We check, because it's important.

Our factory is also a small family business. It is run by a couple, and our main point of contact is their son. The cutters and sewers are extended family and friends, and they take care of each other.

How is SWISH manufacturing done?

Our fabrics are ordered directly through the factory, and through a few companies in Montreal who work strictly with the mills. Our patterns are drafted jointly by Lynn and a Vancouver-based pattern making company when the volume gets to be too much for one set of hands to handle, and then Lynn oversees all components of production.

When an order is placed, a marker must be ordered from the patternmakers. A marker is a pattern that includes all sizes for a style. The marker is then provided with a sample, fabric and an order to the factory. From the point of ordering, it takes between 6 and 8 weeks to complete. From the factory, the clothes go straight to the store, ready for your next visit. That's why we always have new stock and new styles – the factory delivers every week.

Chapter Four: Display

Our displays get lots of compliments and the first question most people ask is who does them?

The right answer is all our staff work constantly at maintaining the beautiful stories our displays tell. When you want a scarf we have as part of a display, the staff will refill and rearrange to fill the space left behind.

It's when we decide to redo our colour theme and shift things around that the story becomes "a work in progress" (we say).

First we plan where the colours all go; this when we engineer the 'big' picture... Next it's the construction phase configuring the walls and furniture... and then we all become the 'interior decorators', tidying the vases, labelling shoe sizes and replenishing stock.

We have the most fun when the store is torn apart, and the display pieces are in baskets and waiting for a new shelf space. We move colour sections around the store every couple of months. We do that so we can tell a new story. If you have one of our tunics and we can show you a new way to wear it, a new way to pair it, or a new scarf to accessorize it, then you'll want to wear that piece over and over again, therefore wearing it out, not throwing it out. And that is how SWISH defines slow fashion!

Something that you'll wear over and over because our displays showed you how, or inspired you to try something different.

Why are all your clothes displayed with scarves and jewelry?

We want to inspire you to look your best and if we can show you different combinations to wear, or how to add a pop of colour or mix patterns, then maybe you'll try something new.

Clothing's main function is to cover us and protect us from the elements but in Western culture, for women, it's an artform, a way to express ourselves. Culturally, we 'read' each other as soon as we 'see' each other and long before a word is spoken. How we feel about ourselves is communicated by what you wear in many ways. Think of meeting your girlfriend for lunch, and she shows up in dirty clothes, dirty hair, needs a shower, and probably some sleep. Unless she has a newborn – in which case she probably needs sleep and a hug! – you'd ask her immediately, "what is wrong?" If you met that same girlfriend and she was well put together, her clothes flattered her, she had a pretty scarf and necklace on, she was rested and sitting tall. You'd probably tell her she looked great and ask her what's new?

How you dress communicates much about how you feel about yourself and leads people in how you want them to react to you.

Why do you put scarves and jewelry on all your displays?

Inspiration! At SWISH, we want you to think, "I can do that."

We use our scarves and jewelry to display finished outfits. We want you to leave the store with an outfit, know what you're going to wear and how you're going to wear it. We want to make it easy to dress and love to hear you say, "I can do that". We also like to hear you say you have pieces already that you could use to get the same look. We believe that if we show you more than one way to use our clothes and accessories, you'll wear your clothes out, and not throw them out.

Husbands, partners, friends, we love it when they come in, see an outfit already put together and say, "This is her style." We love sending them home successful and feeling accomplished.

Why do you merchandise by colour?

When you walk into SWISH, there's a lot to take in, so we colour block. We think it makes the store feel smaller. If you wear blue, but not red, then you can stay in the blue section and skip the red section. If you're looking to match something you already have, then you don't have to walk the whole store looking for it because we've organized the clothes and accessories to help you save time and it helps us find what you need quickly when you ask for help. Another reason we colour block is because we want to show you how the clothes work together. How to put different pieces together with different prints and solids, scarves and accessories so you go home with a complete outfit and you know how to wear it.

Think about how easy it would be to dress in the morning, if your wardrobe was organized the same way! All your blues with your blues, outfits organized. You'd never open the doors and lament, "I have nothing to wear!" Instead, you'd have to struggle with what to choose!

Chapter Five: The Design Process

Typically trends start in Europe and move to the east coast of North America, namely New York, Montreal, and Toronto. Then they migrate to the west coast, LA and then travel north.

With social media and the internet the speed of fashion is just a blur – or is it?

Fast Fashion: Runway to hanger in 2 weeks. Fast Fashion is namely Joe Fresh, Zara, H&M and Topshop.

They can see the design on the runway and have it hanging in their stores worldwide in 2 weeks.

> Designed
> Sewn
> Shipped
> Hung ---- 2 weeks

Ethical manufacturing – not even close.

At SWISH we have a 4-part design process:

- Wholesale
- Retail
- Street Fashion
- Adaptation

Our design team (namely Lynn and Katy) researches the design marketplace 4-6 times per year. Our first stop is at the wholesale level where we look for common details between manufacturers. Then we check out the retail stores to see which style lines are strongest and what major retailers believe to be important to the season.

And before we go to the design room we look at what people are buying and which trend they are comfortable with.

Then we listen. We listen to you. You are, after all, the expert on the upcoming trends because if you won't buy sleeveless tops there's no point making them – that trend will die.

So we look and we listen and then we follow your direction with a little NYC thrown in for fun. We also work on a North American fit, because we're curvy, and we've had a few birthdays.

Chapter Six: Fabric

A t SWISH, we choose our fabrics very carefully, and we tend to play favourites.

The two most used fabrics in our line are modal and bamboo, and these are very versatile and wearable fabrics for a multitude of reasons. But, we'll get to that. In order to understand these two heavy hitters, we have to talk about Rayon.

It all starts with Rayon. Rayons are natural, manufactured fibres. Confused already? Ok, let's break it down. Rayon is a natural fibre, because at the base of everything, it's made from wood cellulose, if you want to be really specific. Rayon is a manufactured fibre, because, unlike cotton, you can't just harvest cellulose, brush it, spin it and say "TADA, yarns!" In order to get a Rayon yarn, the cellulose of the wood has to be mashed up with some solutions, then pressed through a contraption that looks like a showerhead, called a spinerette, and then doused in another solution to set the fibres. Makes a little more sense now?

Now, I know some people go, "Ew, rayon, it's a SYNTHETIC fibre, yuck." And those people are wrong, because, again, it comes from a natural source. But, similar to synthetics, there is a chemical process that gets us from wood chips to that beautiful scarf you're wearing. The important thing to note here is that this process has been adapted and enhanced immensely since these fabrics were introduced; the processes have become environmentally friendly, and the fabrics have evolved to be superior in many ways to many natural fibres (don't worry cotton/linen/etc, we still love you!)

Because Rayon is a semi-natural fibre, it does still share some characteristics with natural cellulose fibres (we're talking about cotton and linen again, here!), but with some engineered advantages (oh, science!). Rayon is more moisture absorbent than cotton, it has a softer hand, making it more comfortable to wear, it drapes nicely and takes dye like a champ (meaning you get a wider, more vivid array of colours). Rayons don't build static (they don't stick to your skin), and they're pill-resistant, so your clothes will always look new! This is also a great choice for peri-menopausal, menopausal, and just women with a high natural body temperature, as it doesn't insulate body heat, so your skin gets a much needed breath of fresh air!

Also, because Rayons are so versatile, they're often mixed with other fabrics to add these wonderful characteristics to blended fibres! But, blended Rayons are also a great thing for washing strength and maintaining garment shape, as Rayons tend to be a little delicate. Spandex does just the trick, and a Rayon/Spandex blend is resilient enough for the washing machine (but please wash cold, to be safe!) and helps beautiful rayons maintain their shape.

Ok, now you know Rayon, let's talk about Modal.

Modal is a Rayon made specifically from the cellulose of beech trees. Why does that make it special? We're glad you asked!! Different wood gives rayon different properties. In addition to the typical characteristics of Rayon, Modal has been developed to be extra soft, to resist creasing, and have a very smooth and lustrous finish. It's both absorbent and very breathable, so it is cool to the touch, and is much stronger when wet than traditional Rayons, making washing very easy and worry-free.

What about Bamboo?

If you had to guess, I'm sure you could figure out that Rayon of Bamboo is a Rayon made from the cellulose of Bamboo! And, again, Bamboo has lots of extra advantages, in addition to all the great things Rayons can already do!

Bamboo is naturally anti-bacterial, anti-fungal (meaning it doesn't hold odours), UV protective (great for the beach!), anti-static (doesn't stick to your skin), breathable and cool, as well as strong, flexible and, like modal, very lustrous.

Another important point, Bamboo fabrics are very eco-friendly, as they're made from a virtually inexhaustible source. Bamboo is a widely grown plant, and some species can grow as much as 3 feet per day! Additionally, Bamboo fabrics are biodegradable, so once you wear your clothes out, Mother Earth will do the rest!

Washing safely.... Every washing machine works differently. Some run hotter than others, some spin tighter than others, some are gentler than others. It's impossible to guess whether "warm" is exactly X degrees or Y degrees, and you'll never know the exact % of water than will get spun out. You'll never know how wet your clothes are going into the dryer, and how hard your dryer will work to combat that moisture. The only real constant in a washer and dryer is that cold water is cold, definitely. So, we always recommend that you wash your clothes in cold water.

With all natural fibres, if you "cook" them in the dryer, they'll lose shape and elasticity. So, that's why we always recommend that you air dry flat. And why flat, you ask? Because, again, you don't know how much weight your clothes have picked up getting wet in that washing machine, and if you hang that beauty up, you run the risk of all that extra water weight pulling down and stretching the shoulders out.

To recap, wash cold, air dry flat. You can thank us later.

Chapter Seven: The Change Room is Therapy

Why do clothes matter? For basic reasons: warmth and protection from the elements, of course, but for women especially, it's more than that. It's an expression of who we are. Our personalities shine through how we dress and how we put our clothes together is an artform.

Clothes give us confidence and will amplify how we want to feel about ourselves and how we want others to relate to us.

Clothes make a powerful statement about who we are.

Why do women shop?

Beyond the obvious, because they need clothes, women shop for entertainment. We enjoy the colour and texture, the possibility and potential.

Where would I wear this? How would this look on me? How would I put this outfit together? All of the potential wardrobe questions take on the job of self expression. It's how our personalities are expressed and it displays how we feel about ourselves.

We talked about why we dress our hangers and create hangers to become outfits. It's for entertainment, to show possibilities, to encourage interpretation. To inspire.

Let's talk about Carol:

Carol came in excited to find a new outfit for a Christmas party. She chose some beautiful tops that she thought would look great with her new black dress pants and headed for the change room. Lynn offered to go and get her other sizes or colours if she needs to, like she does with all SWISH customers – the worst is when you have to go looking for a different size in your sock feet, wearing store clothes that don't fit or else having to put all your own clothes back on again, just to get all undressed again after trying to find another size! Ugh, agony!

Carol started to get very quiet and wasn't coming out to look in the big 3-way mirror (the runway of our changerooms). When asked if she needed anything, she said she was ok, but her tone and lack of enthusiasm made it very clear that that wasn't the case. It was time to figure out what was going on...

In near tears, she emerged from the change room, reluctantly, in a top that look beautiful, but, she was very obviously not happy.

After talking to Lynn for a few minutes, Carol revealed that she had recently lost 100lbs. She was proud of herself, and happy with the results, but when she looked in the mirror, she felt shy and vulnerable and wanted to hide in the safe volume of her baggy clothes. She also shared that her mean sister-in-law was going to be at the Christmas party, and she was worried that she would be subjected to rude comments like she had been in the past. Carol didn't have any desire to even go to this party.

Lynn asked if she could give it a shot, and see if she could find something that made her feel safe, but also beautiful and confidence, so that, if anyone wanted to make a comment, it would be a compliment! And, even if mean sister-in-law had something rude to say, sorry, but screw you, mean sister-in-law, that's not what sisterhood is about.

They talked about the top she had chosen, and why it worked so well for her. Her eyes sparkled against the right shade of blue, and the cut followed her small frame and draped at just the right spot on her ribcage. When we focused on Carol's assets, and pointed out how the style flattered her, she started to smile.

"Okay, now let's make it safe!" announced Lynn, as she pulled a few more pieces and sent Carol back into the changeroom for the finishing touches.

When Carol emerged once again from the change room, she was radiant. In addition to the top she had chosen for herself, Lynn had added a soft linen vest, a silk scarf, and a long silver necklace. Now, there was an outfit! And the best accessory of all? Confidence. Not only did Carol look fantastic, she KNEW it. The vest and scarf added an extra layer, so she wasn't feeling exposed, and therefore had no instinctual need to hide, and the necklace highlighted the blues of her top and eyes. Instant stunner!

And, through this process, Carol realised she didn't need the weight of her baggy clothes to feel safe. She could be strong and healthy and confident, and use her wardrobe to get her there.

Of course, she rocked the heck out of that party. She realised that no one could take away her weight loss success and she basked in the compliments she received that night.

Carol sent Lynn an email a few months after the party, thanking Lynn for her help. She also reported that she had met her new boyfriend at the Christmas party! And, his first comment was to tell her how much he liked her outfit... they've been together for over a year now.

Oh, and there was no mention of any rude comments from her mean sister-in-law!

Chapter Eight: Screw "appropriate"

L ynn worked for years in the garment industry, and she was told, from time to time, to dress more "appropriately". This was also a problem for Katy, who, as a twenty-something with a large chest and an affinity for high heels, struggled to find office-"appropriate" clothing that would be inoffensive to her much more conservative boss.

But, going through these experiences, it became more and more obvious to both women that clothing matters. What you put on your body changes how you feel about yourself, and therefore, how you present yourself to the world. People react to that. When you feel confident, others are attracted to that inner confidence, that inner strength, and you have power in any situation.

So, before we address the idea of clothing identity, let's tackle one thing: what is "appropriate"? The answer, in most cases, is WHO THE HECK CARES?! With the exception of situations where a dresscode is imposed (galas, offices, private schools... etc.), there are really no rules. Society likes to tell us to dress for our age, weight, height, blah blah blah. If you love it, and you feel hot as hell in it, it's appropriate. You want to rock the crop top? Rock the damned crop top. You look amazing!

Ok, moving on... Clothing identity, or: Whose body is this anyway!?

As we grow up, we go through some stages of self-discovery, and this can often affect our style! For example...

Teen-25: Who am I and who do I want to be?

These girls are hugely influences by celebrities and social media. It's an age of trying things and experimenting. Because this stage is so transitional your closet will be an eclectic mix, lots of experimentation and finding out who you are.

25-35 student – professional – motherhood

How do I juggle all of this?!?!!??! And how do I find time to dress for every situation? This is the stage that basics became your best friend and accessories became your way to adapt to any situation.

45-55 premenopausal – menopausal aka whose body is this anyway??

This stage of life brings on its own challenges. Because our bodies are changing and we're not sure how to dress, we can't wear what we've always worn because we're not comfortable with our new bodies.

55-65

The kids have left home, I spend my time differently and I can make different choices with how I spend my time and money. For the first time in a long time, I get to ask, "What do I want for ME?"

65++ Retirement

This stage of dressing is really interesting and really important. This transition has the biggest shift in identity. The closet built for a career needs to be recreated for retirement.

Let's meet Susan! Susan, come on down!

Susan and three of her closest girlfriends came in after checking in for their girls getaway at a B&B in Gibsons Landing, close to the water, and close to the liquor store! One of the girls, Linda, shared that they had kidnapped Susan for a weekend away, but they were vague about the reason why.

Being a group of ladies shopping, they were a pretty self-sufficient group, and Lynn's input was minimal and practical, but she mostly stood back and let them have fun! After about 90 min of trying on and fashion shows to the oohs and ahhs of the other girls, they walked out of the shop, each swinging a bag of treasures! They were taking their retail therapy seriously! As they were stepping out to explore the rest of the town, Linda pulled Lynn aside to explain that the reason for the getaway was that Susan had just found out her husband of 5 years had been having an affair throughout their marriage. Thank goodness for girlfriends, am I right? Yikes!

The next morning, the group returned, though a little less lively than the afternoon before. In slightly hushed voices, they explained that the wine had flowed a little freely the night before, and they were a little... headachey. As they moved around the store, they were less enthusiastic, and Lynn asked if she could give it a try, and suggest some things. Yes! They were happy to have someone else do the work today.

Lynn pulled two or three hangers for each of the girls, but paid special attention to Susan. She brought over a top that she knew would be a perfect look for Susan. Susan took a look at the top, looked at Lynn, then back at the top and said it was something she would never have chosen for herself. Lynn just smiled and told her to give it a try. Time for a little retail magic.

With a hangover, a little faith and nothing to lose, Susan went into the changeroom. The woman who burst through the curtains a few minutes later was a completely different person. The top was a beautiful mix of strong blues, the same colour as her eyes, and a bit of sheen mixed with white. It showed off her flawless skin and beautiful colouring to its best.

Susan stood in front of the mirror, silent, staring. She turned to Lynn and said, "I'd have never picked this."

"I know," said Lynn with a smile.

With the magic that happens when you come out of the change room in clothes that bring out what's best about you, it's easy to find your strength, your power, your potential. Susan saw this in an instant.

After the shock of finding out the last 5 years of her life weren't what she thought they were, she had been shaken, but when she saw herself at her best in front of that mirror, she knew she wouldn't be a victim of the last 5 years, but a champion in the face of a challenge.

Susan took her time celebrating her newfound strength with her friends, and then she changed back into her own clothes, gathered up her new pieces, including the "I'd never have picked that" top, and headed to the cash counter. En route, she stopped and said to Lynn, again, that she never would have picked that top out. She explained about her husband and why they came up for the weekend, tears in her eyes.

Lynn told her, "If you tried on a top that you never would have tried, what else can you do that you never tried?"

She looked at Lynn for a moment, and said, "You don't just sell clothes here." Lynn gave her a knowing smile and nodded, "We don't just sell clothes here."

Susan sent an email a few months later. Because she was able to shift her view of herself and what she was capable of, she had closed the doors on her marriage, bought her first house by herself, and enrolled in art school, something she had put off for years.

Chapter Nine: Start your wardrobe from the inside out

Yep, we're talking about bras, undies, and lingerie, ladies! One of the first comments we get when you head to the changeroom? "I'm wearing the wrong bra..." (Honestly, we're thrilled if you're wearing one at all!) Instinctively, we know when a bra is past its prime (but it's just so damned comfortable!)

Secrets of the bra industry (or not such a big secret afterall...): Bra companies want you to buy more bras, more often. No surprise there, but really, a bra, properly fitted, should last you 2 years if your body stays the same.

Bra fitting 101

Them Vs. Us

Hook your bra on the middle hooks Vs. Hook your bra on the most open hooks

Wear your bra until it goes in the laundry Vs. Give it 2 days rest between wearing to rest the elastic

Refit every 6 months Vs. If you haven't changed weight, refit every year, and if your bras are still in good shape and pass the "fit test" then spend your money on something fun like a new scarf instead!

5 Fit Tips

There are 5 things to look for when you fit a bra. If you're at the store getting fitted, don't let yourself get talked into a style or size unless these 5 points are addressed and you feel comfortable.

1) Face the mirror – nothing spills over the cup. Most of us have breasts that are different sizes. Always fit for your fuller side. You can adjust your strap to ease spillage, if that doesn't work then go to a larger cup size.
2) The triangle between the cups (called the "centerfront gore') should fit tight to your breast bone. If it pulls away, you need a larger cup size (and usually a smaller band)
3) Lift your arms over your head. If the band moves away from your ribcage, and you can see a gap between you and your bra, your band is too big. Go to a smaller band size and bigger cup size.
4) Stand sideways to the mirror – the fullest part of your breast should sit halfway between the top of your shoulder and the bottom of your elbow.
5) The band in the back should be horizontal to the ground. If your band curves up like a sunrise, your breasts will sit lower in front. You need a smaller band and a larger cup.

What's the big deal?

When you're positioned properly, the line from your breastbone to your bellybutton is longer, and longer = thinner. It's an instant 5lb weight loss... Try it! Look in the mirror and hunch your shoulders so your become shorter from your breastbone down. Now stand tall. See the difference? Get those girls up there where they belong! It'll perk you up! (pun fully intended!)

What about back fat?

Yep, we've all got it. Happy Birthday! When you put your bra on and dress, be sure to pull the sides up and over your bits, don't let the soft spots spill over. More times than not we create the problem by not lifting the band and tucking in.

Why a molded cup?

- It evens out your breasts, if you're two sizes
- Nipple coverage (in case it gets a little chilly)
- You take on the shape of the bra

Why a soft cup?

- Feels more like you... if you're two sizes, a molded cup bra could feel "bigger" because it's evened out your small side.
- You give the bra shape so it feels more natural

Types of Bras

T-shirt Bra–As the name suggests, **t-shirt bras are perfect for wearing under anything tight, close-fitting, or thin.** Because the bra is constructed of one seamless piece, you won't end up with those annoying boob-shaped lines under your clothes. In addition, the molded cups make them great for evening and shaping the breasts without adding padding or bulk.

nude Bra--**When you want to wear light or white-colored clothing, a nude bra is a wardrobe essential**. Many people equate nude with one beige or tan shade, but, in reality, nude is whatever matches your skintone.

Convertible Bra–Because not all your clothing has sleeves or straps, you need a convertible bra. The best convertible bras are able to accommodate strapless, halter, and low-back styles with some brands even having crisscross or one shoulder options. To maximize flexibility, also look for a bra with a deep, plunging front, perfect for v-necks and scoopnecks.

Panties

When it comes to panties, the default style is seamless. No matter if you like briefs or boyshorts, thongs or bikinis... seamless is the way to go.

Not all fabrics are created equal. You need a variety of fabrics to do different jobs. Nylon or slippery fabric panties are for when you want your clothes to slide. A slinky dress or a floating palazzo pant when you want no resistance to let the fabric slide. On the other hand you don't want your jeans slipping to the floor so cotton panties will hold firmer and grip the fabric so you have a better chance of not having to hike up your jeans as you're walking down the street!!

As a final step, double check that you have been caring for your underwear properly. The first step to good garment care, as basic as it sounds, is to actually follow the instructions on the label, i.e. don't wash something at 40 degrees if the limit on the label is 30 and hand wash if an item needs to be hand washed. Beyond that, simply stick to a few best practices: Never tumble dry your underwear or leave it on the radiator. Always let it dry naturally. Make sure bras lie flat when drying or are hung from the gore (i.e. the center part that connects the cups), never from the straps. Always hand wash lacy, delicate items and avoid hot temperatures. It's also a good idea to put items that can be machine-washed in a laundry mesh bag. This will prevent other garments from getting tangled in bra hooks or the underwiring and, more importantly, also reduce the strain on the garments inside (they are not tossed over as much) and thereby prevent them from losing shape.

Chapter Ten: How to get out of your fashion rut

C olour – not just black. Black is our go to. We feel smaller, it hides our soft bits and perceived flaws. Black absorbs light, so the light isn't bounced back and there's no emphasis on the soft bits we want to ignore. White, by contrast, bounces light like a pro and there are no secrets.

In terms of economic uncertainty, black is a safe investment. Watch the colour focus in the stores when there's political unrest or if the economy is headed to, or already in, a recession. Black will never go out of style, it's easy to update, and basics can last year after year, so buy quality. BUT!

It's boring as HELL. Where's your personality? How are you going to shine through? We don't want to lose you in the shadows.

If you like colour and black plays a minor role in your wardrobe, read on anyways, you can help encourage the masses!

How your colouring changes as you have more birthdays – don't get stuck in your "season" from the 80's

Colour Me Beautiful™ was a colour draping concept in the 80's. It was the first time women dictated colour to the fashion industry instead of being told what was in this year. If you weren't a summer and your shade of pink wasn't part of the year's pallet, the fashion industry lost you as a customer for the season. But, there were a couple of limitations when using this concept. We've had women come through the store with their "swatches" and if our blue was a shade or two off, then they'd walk away, saying, "It's not my blue!" That kind of thinking starts to limit your choices because there are many shades of a colour and lots to choose from.

Another limitation is that colours change and are mixed differently all the time. Fabrics hold dyes differently; technology has advanced hugely since the 80's. Don't get stuck in a colour rut because of a set of rules developed 40 years ago.

A few birthdays can change everything.

- As we collect more birthdays (which we highly recommend doing!) our colouring changes. Most obvious is hair colour (love those Arctic highlights!) but our skintone, teeth and eye colour all change too.

So how do you pick your colour? Try the pinch test. Everyone has an underlying skin tone, and this will help you to be more informed in choosing colours. Pinch the skin on the back of your hand, your earlobe, or your fingertip, and the underlying colour will be shown for a few seconds. Is your undertone blue, rosy pink or red violet? You'll likely do better with cooler colours. Is your tone more golden, peach, coral or warm red? You'll likely do better in warmer colours.

Universally flattering colours

- Purple
- Teal

Warm

- Gold
- Plum
- Brown

Cool

- Silver
- Blue
- White

Here's a challenge. Go into a store with lots of colour options, find a style you like, and try it in all ALL the colours. Which colour do you feel best in? How do you like your skintone, eye colour, etc?

Body type – use clothes to balance and emphasize your assets

Yes, you have assets, so quit looking for flaws. You're perfect, remember?

It's our theory that if clothes can make you look 50lbs heavier, we should be able to make you look 50lbs lighter. Draw attention to what you like about your appearance and quit finding things to worry about.

On a scale of 0-5 (5 being LOVE LOVE LOVE) rate your features:

Hair – style

Hair – colour

Eyes

Facial features

Chinline

Neck

Shoulders

Breasts

Ribcage

Waistline

Hips

Legs

Feet

Height

If there aren't SOME 5's in there, we're going to pour us both some wine and take you out back for a stern talk. This is just between you and you. Go back and look over the list and BE KIND.

Ask yourself, if that was my best friend in the mirror, instead of myself, would I be nearly so critical? No, of course not! But remember, that IS your best friend in the mirror. She's the one who will be with you to the end, no matter what. BE KIND TO HER.

Most women will like their facial features – yes, some parts more than others – but that's where your character is. In your eyes, your smile, your sparkle!

When we're at the changeroom and you're focussed on what bugs you generally, we start complaining from the ribcage down. Rarely does anyone fuss over their shoulders or ribcage. If we focus on these areas, we can draw attention up and let the rest take care of itself.

When you choose colour, look to highlight your eyes, they don't call them the windows to the soul for nothing!!

When you're looking for colours and have gone to the changeroom with the earlier challenge (a top you like in every colour), what impact does that colour have on your eyes and skintone?

If you love your body, we applaud you! We congratulate and cheer you on! You figured it out, and you're RIGHT! You're perfect and the world needs to know! If you're still trying to figure out your changing body (see chapter 8) then let's break it down. Ignore body issues by dressing shoulders and ribcage.

Lots of women going through childbirth, peri-menopause or menopause find breast size changes, middles thicken, weight gets added or lost or just redistributed.

The reality is you're still perfect, but it just doesn't feel like you. So, we need to redefine your comfort zone.

And how exactly do I do THAT?!?

Clean shoulder to ribcage

Your clothes sit clean to your body (no folds or bulky fabric) at the shoulder.

J hook under the breast

Fabric comes down clean to your breast, and gives a slight shadow underneath (something like a "J")

Screen and a clean silhouette

A clean silhouette is something like a cami that sits close to your body.

Create a screen with a sheer top

A screen is a sheer garment that goes over top, so you shine through, but your lumps and bumps have been smoothed out and can be ignored.

Your sleeve length should draw your eye to where you're small, or where you want to emphasize.

- ¾ sleeve should point to a tiny waist
- A short sleeve should point to a tiny ribcage
- A long sleeve should never match a horizontal hemline

The best way to direct the eye is by angling the hemline, no matter the length, and you can do that by: folding back the sleeve, or using a button buddy.

Horizontal lines and stripes

Horizontal lines: Whether it's a stripe or a hem, the eye will play the horizontal line the same way, and you want to keep that line short. Take the high/low hem, for example (genius, by the way!).

Pop on a cami underneath, and pull it up so the high/low top cuts off the edges of the cami hem. This shortens the line of the cami, and your eye will naturally think that your hip line is the same length as that shorter line. Magic, no?

Horizontal lines and stripes

Stripes work the same way. If you wear a thick rugby stripe that goes straight across your body, you're going to look the full length of that stripe; there's nothing there to break the lines up. If you work with thinner stripes, broken stripes, paneled garments that mix stripes and other fabrics, or clothes that drape and fold, you eye will cut every time that stripe line is interrupted, making you look skinnier.

Great legs and garment length

"Great legs" aren't one-size-fits-all. You don't have to have long, tanned, thin legs to have "great legs." A great leg is proportionate to the body and tapers from hip to ankle (and then, hopefully, ends in a foot). Take a look at your leg, and find the spot where that taper starts (it's usually somewhere on the thigh). This is your "sweet spot" and that is where your tunics should end. This way, you start with your clean lines up at the shoulder, "J" hook around your breast, then float away down to your "sweet spot" and you miss everything in the middle. Because we start showing leg at the "sweet spot," you look thinner, and that trend continues down the line of the leg, as it tapers more down to the ankle.

Assymetrical hemline and camis

This works a lot like the high/low concept. Because you have an assymetrical line, you pull your hem up so that the hem line is cut off by the assymetrical hem, and you get that skinny hip in a whole new way.

Assymetrical stylelines

When a top has asymmetrical style lines, it works like broken stripes. All the lines on the garment break up the space on our body, and you look smaller.

Scarves

A scarf redefines your jawline – the scoop of a cowl from a scarf reframes the jaw, mirrors the curve of the jawline, and makes your jaw look sharper.

Screen

Create a waterfall – tie a knot at about breastbone level, then turn the scarf so it sits assymetrically to one side. This waterfall effect floats away from the body and creates another screen. This is a great trick if you're worried about your middle.

Jewelry

Earrings should be proportionate to your neck length. If you have a short neck, stick with short earrings. The earring will draw attention up to your face, and when you draw the eye upwards, you give the illusion of extra height. This will also highlight the eyes!

Necklaces

Necklaces: just like your hands, your upper chest ages. A necklace will help diffuse age spots and make you look younger. A long necklace will create a V-shaped neckline, draws attention up, reframe jawline to look younger. The length of the v needs to be proportionate to height as well, so keep the point of the V just below your breast bone.

Why do you care? Jewelry will add the third dimension to your clothing, which is the sparkle, light bouncing off, reflection. We'll tell you more later in chapter 12, but remember, this is important. You care, we promise.

How do I make the most of my choices?

The more ways you can wear your clothes, the more likely you'll wear your clothes out instead of throwing them out, and that's our definition of slow fashion (remember chapter 5).

Can you wear that top/tunic over pants/capris /jeans/skirts/basic dress? Can you pair it more ways than the way it was presented on the hanger?

We have a great top that you'd naturally wear with a pant, capri or jean, but put it over our basic t-shirt dress (weekend splash), or the LBD that's been in your closet forever (great staple, by the way), suddenly it has better range and it will become your go to whether it's shopping with the girls, or out to dinner with you know who (wink, wink).

We call this range. The greater the range a garment has, the more likely you'll wear it more often, so start looking at your pieces a little differently, and ask yourself how else you can wear it.

Our poncho is a great example. Visit our facebook page (facebook.com/swishladieswear) and we'll show you 11 ways to wear it, transitioning from accessories to clothing!

Can you change the colour focus with different accessories?

If you have a solid top, add a printed scarf, or if you have a printed top, add a solid scarf to highlight a different colour within the print. Your accessories are a great and easy tool.

Don't forget your cami! Try changing this layering piece, and you can add a pop of colour under a lower neckline or extend a hemline in the same way.

Can you change the range of the garment from casual to dressy by how you pair it or layer it?

Try that top over a dress (LBD, as mentioned before) or can you change a hemline with a button buddy (again, check out our Facebook page).

Can you change the layers?

Revisit that cami or poncho or dress... or... or... or... the possibilities are endless!

Can you go from season to season with a few add-ons?

Layering is a change of season's best friend! Remember, you can add layers both under and over a garment. A sleeveless tunic can welcome cooler temperatures with a t-shirt under or a cardi over, or have you discovered Sleevey Wonder™? It's genius!

A sheer sleeve, either mesh or lace that goes under a sleeveless top to cover your arms for: a style change, to keep you covered if this is an area that concerns you, or to add a light layer of warmth in case it gets chilly.

The brilliance of a sleeveless garment is that you can add or subtract as needed.

Leggings!

A wardrobe staple, but do you really need a wardrobe of various lengths? No! Use your button buddy to adjust length and add style and interest.

Button buddies are genius too with a ¾ length sleeve! Shorten you sleeve with a button buddy for a style and season change.

For a button buddy lesson, check out our facebook page (again: Facebook.com/swishladieswear)

Ok, let's talk about those "flaws"!

Honestly, we hate focusing here, but maybe if we have the conversation, we can put it in perspective and move on....

Arms: Arms are probably the #1 most disliked body part! Really? Look at what they do for you! All day! And just think of how many friends they've hugged or how many babies they've held. They spread a lot of love, so let's make friends!

In Chapter 12 we'll talk about screens (don't worry, we'll get there) and Sleevey Wonder will provide that effect without overpowering your outfit or adding a layer over, like when you use a poncho or a wrap a scarf as a shawl. Think past a cardigan or sleeved top. Add style when you add coverage and think past a sleeve as the only solution.

Chest: It doesn't matter if you think you have too much or too little, this is a sensitive area. For small-busted girls, add volume with draped or ruched necklines, cowls, and princess or empire lines that emphasize your ribcage.

If you're trying to minimize, then a modified empire line that curves just under the bust, but not all the way to the ribcage is good. Any top that gives you that perfect "J" hook. Try a V neck, or create one with your button buddy and play with diagonal lines to break up the space.

Tummy: It's funny how we expect to have a flat stomach even when our bodies go through a natural change process. Our tummy is a birthday present! It has food stores in case of illness or famine. It's your stores THAT WILL KEEP YOU ALIVE! That doesn't mean you're going to start eating cookies morning, noon and night, but if you do add a few inches here, say thank you! It may just be what you need to get back to good health!

But – this doesn't mean you can't be smarter than an extra inch or two...

Where your tummy decides to have a way of its own (we call this an apron) position the hem of your cami here, layer a high/low top so the cami just pokes out at the hemline. The crease of your apron will be blamed on your cami and your rounded tummy will, by illusion, flatten and the curve of the high/low hem will shrink the roundness. This is another example of engineered design. Using lines, curves and placement to re-educate the eye to see what we want it to see.

Hips and Thighs: We've already covered this one. Camis and high/low hems, assymetrical hems, and finding the "sweet spot" with your garment length, and you are SET, my friend! NEXT!

How we talk to ourselves

I hate my _____!! Katy and Lynn were taking the subway in New York (we know what you're thinking, Lynn's a cab-only girl, but this was a one-off) and there was a display of posters showing the work of Masaru Emoto, who photographed the effect that words have on water (remember the human body is 60% water). They took microscopic photos while playing different music or saying different words to the water during the freezing process. The result? When they said kind words to the water, they produced beautiful crystals, but when they said unkind words to the water, the crystals always came out deformed and damaged. Think twice about what you say to yourself when you look in the mirror... Be kind!

Love & Gratitude

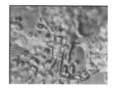

You disgust me

(Source http://www.masaru-emoto.net/english/water-crystal.html)

Chapter Eleven: How to use fabrics

W hy do you colour block? Look in your closet. What's the dominant colour? Is that your favourite colour? Why did you choose those pieces? Sale? Love it? Only thing that fit? How do you feel in it? Does it highlight your: skin, hair, eyes? Change your clothes, change your life.

Change 1 thing.

Power of colour

Accessories

Jewelry and scarves – draw attention up to your face, highlight eyes, skin, and/or hair!

Prints – When rocking prints, you want to look for something with minimal background space. The more space showing, the bigger you look, so look for bold prints!

Assets

Raise the waistline – Don't forget your "J" hook.

Length – hit your hemlines at the "sweet spot" on your leg.

Look for a vertical element to keep the eye traveling up and up, which makes you look taller and slimmer.

Tunics – do I look pregnant? Not if that "J" hook is part of the picture!!

Chapter Twelve: Building a wardrobe

O k, so now you know what colours to look for, how we style clothes to highlight your best features, and that you're allowed to break the rules. Now what? We bet the big question on your mind is...

Where do I start?

As with anything, you start with the foundation. We've tackled the bra problem, and now you're looking sexy as heck underneath anything you put on, but how do we up the ante and get the whole package together?

Parisian ladies (considered some of the most fashionable by many) rely heavily on a capsule wardrobe to look flawless for little to no effort. What is a capsule wardrobe, you ask? A capsule wardrobe is a very small collection of highly useful clothing that forms the base of your wardrobe, working hard from season to season. Having a capsule wardrobe in place means you know your ass is covered (literally), and it's easily updated season to season with a few key pieces and accessories, so you always look current and put together.

SWISH Definition: we want you to have a few "hangers" and many outfits. Our capsule wardrobes move from season to season depending on how you layer your pieces and how you use your accessories. The key to our clothing is how you can update your wardrobe season to season, but also year to year. With small add-ons, you can take last year's choices and update your look without having to reinvent and reinvest in a whole new wardrobe every year.

But, a capsule wardrobe is not one-formula-fits-all solution. We need to figure out what capsule works for your life (do you opt for sophisticated or the casual?)

So, let's learn about you! What do you do? If you work in a bank and host fancy dinner parties, you might need cocktail dresses and suits. Alternately, if you are a stay-at-home mom, and chase kids around all day, a blazer and dress pant is probably not going to be a part of your capsule.

And, beyond work, how do you spend your time? Do you love to do yoga at sunrise? Do you live for walks on the beach, or is your idea of a great afternoon curling up on the couch with a glass of wine and a good book? These are all factors that will affect your capsule.

Here's a little questionnaire to see what kind of lifestyle you need to dress for:

What do you do?

- Work
- Weekends
- Hobbies
- Travel
- Entertaining

What styles do you most wear?

- Classic
- Business
- Cutting Edge
- Trendy
- Country
- Casual
- Athletic
- Boho
- Romantic

What do you most look for when purchasing clothing? (Circle all that apply!)

- Fit
- Style
- Trend
- Fits your lifestyle
- Comfort
- Cost
- Travels well
- Versatility

By identifying a few key points, you're able to work through the fog of where to start. Sometimes it all feels like a big job if you're not a shopper and when the trends change so often now with the speed of fast fashion, it can be hard to keep up!

How do I know if it fits? If you have to ask then it probably doesn't – having said that ask yourself these questions:

- Shoulder/ribcage – do you have a clean shoulder and a focus in this area that defines your shape?
- Height – When you look in the mirror do you look tall? Short? Or 'normal'?
- Alterations – Can a little time at the sewing machine give your clothes another chance at fabulous? Find a good alterationalist and your clothes will last longer!

Base piece dressing (these are the pieces you start with) – it's all about how you put the puzzle pieces together

Solid basics + fashion + accessories = an amazing wardrobe on trend and inspiring

You don't have to rebuild your wardrobe every season or every year. The addition of a few good pieces should upgrade your basics from year to year without reinventing your closet from scratch.

Necessary basics (Base pieces to start with):

- Pant
- Capri
- Shirt
- Leggings/jeggings
- T-shirt

Let's get this done!

What you need:

Base piece vs stand alone

A base piece is a versatile piece that mixes well with the rest of your wardrobe.

A stand alone is something you wear exactly as it comes off the hanger, no versatility (it's not work, either, 'cause you'll wear it is as, but it risks being recognized as "that piece again?" because you can really only wear it one way)

Fashion pieces, accessories

Fashion pieces – statement pieces that will bring forward your base pieces, and update them for the season. The more you can layer these pieces, the fewer you'll need without compromising being on trend.

Style lines 20x20

This is the beauty of engineered designed. 20 years younger, 20 lbs lighter. Follow the "rules" when choosing your pieces and you can thank us later.

Height

By illusion, we want to grow by inches. Choose clothes and lines that draw your eye up and make you "taller"

Fit and Design Lines

Trying to hide under a tent of fabric doesn't always make you look thinner. Fit is essential. This doesn't always mean tight, but it does mean drawing your eye to your assets.

Moving from day to evening

By changing your mix, that is, using the same tunic with leggings for day and switching to a layering skirt for evening, you've just increased the range of your tunic and made the transition quick and simple.

Accessories

Sometimes it's as easy as changing your shoes, adding a necklace or scarf, or putting on a wrap to dress things up a bit.

Moving from life stage to life stage

When you move from life stage to life stage, sometimes you need to let go of your old identity and make space for who this new girl is! Until you let go if the clothes that went with the old identity, you can't really evolve. Set new goals and make sure your wardrobe matches!

Weight loss or gain

It happens to all of us. Use your style lines to create what feels more like you.

Season to season

Layering, baby!

Fashion

It's not a spectacular sport but it can be really easy to pull off when you know some basic rules.

Our culture assumes that fashion comes easy for women, in reality it's one of the most intimidating things for many.

We assume all men can change the oil in your car, but the reality is that maybe 10% can. The same assumption goes for women – only about 10% of the female population was born with the fashion gene. The rest struggle with the expectation.

So, we're going to break it down for you because really, once the bombardment of fashion advice is simplified, you can dress fashionably and stress-free.

Ok, here we go:

Step one: Cleaning out your closet

Get 3 boxes

All your clothes will fit into these categories:

1) Throw away – anything damaged/stained
2) Charity – never wore, didn't really fit... But someone else might love it.
3) Favourites that don't fit/haven't worn, but love
4) Things that are great right now, that you wear often and comfortably

Go through your closet and evaluate your clothes. Put them into one of these categories, and into your boxes for categories 1-3, or back in your closet for number 4.

See? That wasn't so terrible!

Now, what do you do with the boxes?

1) Gets thrown in the garbage, or torn into rags to clean the bathroom
2) Donate all of this – if you're on the fence on any of these pieces, toss them in box 3

3) Store these somewhere out of the way – keep them relatively handy, though, you want to be able to quickly and easily find any piece you "miss" and want to wear. Keep them for a year, and if you haven't worn them, they get donated too.

We also have multiple sizes in our closets. If you've lost/gained weight, don't get rid of those clothes just yet – weight changes all through life... Keep your favourites.

4) These are the pieces still in your closet, the ones you love best, and the ones that still fit.

Organize these babies so they're easy to find.

- o Basics – by colour: black, navy, brown
- o Fashion – pieces that are outside of your basic colours, things that are what will make your outfits pop
- o Favourites
- o Stand Alone – pieces that are a basically a whole outfit, and often can only be worn one way

Chapter Thirteen: Why Accessorize?

A ccessories are the polish, the finishing touches to a beautiful outfit. We say, as human beings, we dress in two dimensions. Vertically (head to toe) and horizontally (side to side), but your accessories give you a third dimension.

Look in the mirror with a pair of sweatpants and a plain white shirt, and you'll see your height and width (and probably more width than you'd likely want to show off!) When we add the accessories, we add the third dimension, which is depth, and the inches – as if by magic – will fall away.

Let's do an experiment:

- Into thirds – sides fall away
- Bling = light – highlight center front = sides fall away

Scarves: Beyond the practical use for scarves (to keep us warm), scarves provide an extra layer to compliment, redefine and camouflage.

As we have more birthdays, our jawline softens. A cowl neckline created by a scarf will redefine your jawline, mirroring your bone structure and making you appear younger. Remember, we all want to look 20 years younger? Here's one of your best tools. Slip an infinity scarf over your head, make a figure eight, crossing it at your chest and toss the loop back over your head. Adjust the 2 layers to best mimic your jawline and mirror your bone structure. See the video on our facebook page (facebook.com/swishladieswear)

As well as redefining your jawline, a scarf adds colour, balances your outfit and can also be used as a screen. A screen is something that softens the lumps and bumps and distracts from perceived flaws. Put your scarf over your head, pick up the selvages, just below your breastbone, and tie a reef knot (left over right, right over left). Turn your scarf ¼ turn, so the knot is assymetrical and let the fabric "waterfall" down your centre body line. This trick brings the attention to your center, letting the sides of your silhouette fall unnoticed or, at least, unfocussed on and creating a slimmer, taller line. See the video on our Facebook page: (Facebook.com /swishladieswear)

Scarves balance an outfit.

Most of us have black in our wardrobe. Some of us have mostly black! Scarves add colour, focus and balance.

If black is your wardrobe basic, then add colour with a scarf. Highlight your eye colour to draw attention to your face and away from perceived flaws. As well, scarves will balance your outfit by bringing up colour. If you wear black on the bottom (black pants or leggings, and black footwear), you'll pull the focus down and it will make you look shorter and heavier. Balance the black for a taller impression.

So, let's pretend this is a truth: the taller you are, the thinner you look. We want to give you height. Through engineered design, either with the lines of your clothes, your accessories, or how you put it all together for every perceived inch we can give you, you look 5 pounds lighter – nice diet plan!

We want you to use your clothes to your best advantage. We want you to feel great! Strong and confident, knowing you look great, are comfortable in who you are and showing the world your best self, your confident self.

Chapter Fourteen: Tricks of the trade

B utton Buddy. We invented the button buddy at first as just scarf accessories. We'd use the button buddy to decorate and anchor our scarves and that's why we use such pretty buttons but as we started to play with this new tool we were amazed as to how much we could work and manipulate fabric to 'fix' clothing problems. Sleeves too long – add a button buddy to shorten the sleeve with style and function. If your leggings are full length and you want capris for summer then manipulate the hem and save having to purchase 2 pairs of leggings. Want a V neck – button buddy to the rescue!! And a horizontal hemline is no one's friend unless it's done on purpose and manipulated to stop your eye where you dictate. So how do you use this wonder tool?? Place the button UNDER your fabric/hem and pinch around the button. The button now matches your clothes because it's covered in the garment's fabric. Bring up from under the hem the elastic and wrap the button at least twice to anchor. Play with the placement until you like the look or the length.

Horizontal Hems - Are no one's friend unless you learn to use them to your advantage. Your eye will follow the horizontal line until it reaches the end. We want to shorten the horizontal length by using assymetrical hemlines and shortening the horizontal distance. We can narrow a hip by using a high/low hem or a diagonal hem and having a contrast colour pop out the bottom stopping short of the full hip measurement. Stripes are another way to break a horizontal line. When a narrow stripe breaks because of a seam or fold the eye will stop where the stripe breaks. This puts to rest the idea that stripes make you look heavy when done right they actually make you thinner.

Sleeve length - if you feel that your top is too big check the sleeve length before writing the garment off. If the sleeve is too long the garment will feel too big and sometimes it's just a matter of using a button buddy or if you have an alterationist then have them hem your sleeve to the right length for you. If you're playing with a short sleeve then make sure the hem of the sleeve is positioned right. A full sleeve should angle into your body to point down to your narrow ribcage. A short sleeve should be either above or below your bust line. If it follows your bust line it will make you wider at your fullest part making you look chestier than you really are. Use this to your advantage and adjust your sleeve length accordingly.

Seasonless leggings – button buddy to the rescue!! You can use your button buddy to change the hemline on your leggings by pulling up the length and ruching the excess fabric into a great summer style.

V Necks are harder to make at the factory level than a scoop neck and can sometimes add cost to a garment. By using your button buddy to 'pull' a V neck you can often change the style of a simple scoop neck getting 2 uses out of your shirt, instead of having to buy another top.

Scarf clips - have you ever had trouble with your scarf moving around and looking sloppy?? We use a scarf clip to anchor your scarf to your top so it can't move around. Gather your scarf and clip all layers to the neck edge of your top, your scarf will stay put and you won't be fighting with it because now it's not moving around.

Chunky knits skewers - For loose knits that you want to manipulate we use a disc and a sweater skewer to manipulate the fabric. Pull up the fabric to adjust the length and drape and then place the disc in place to hold all the sweater layers. Twist the sweater skewer down and up inside the disc to secure the fabric.

Let's meet Brenda

Brenda has a closet full of clothes and nothing to wear. She wanted to dress up for her office party but nothing seemed to work. She was frustrated because she had all these clothes at home and still she was shopping for more. She told Lynn about a couple of dresses that she had and liked, but had worn both over the last couple of years, and she liked them, but wanted something new.

It was tricky for Lynn to picture the dresses from Brenda's description, so we agreed that she would come back later in the day and bring them with her.

Upon her return, they headed straight for the changeroom and had a look. Brenda had two very classic dresses, one black and one navy, both beautiful classic cuts that fit her perfectly.

As she put on the black dress, Lynn went hunting for some layering pieces, wraps and accessories. She showed Brenda how they could layer her dress in different ways to take it from sporty casual to glamorous evening depending on how she used the layering pieces, her shoes and boots, and her accessories. Then they did the same with the navy dress.

Brenda went from berating herself for wasting money and making poor purchases to learning how far she could stretch her very savvy clothes plus most everything she had. She hadn't ever been shown how to put it all together.

Because Brenda could spend some time and learn how to layer and accessorize, she was able to feel smart and confident about her choices and save, because she bought smart and less. In fact, she saved enough that she was able to afford a Christmas vacation in Mexico a year earlier than planned.

Chapter Fifteen: Customer Service

D o you have everything you need? When you leave the store, your outfit should be complete, not just another top in your bag. If you need jewelry, a scarf, etc, let's get it all done or let's experiment with enough pieces that you'll inspired to check out your own stuff

Problem Solving 101

Remember, you're perfect! We just focussed on your assets. Are you feeling confident and ready to take on the world. If you're still focussed on what bothers you, it's time to look at it again. Don't be convinced by perceived "flaws", you got this.

Alterations – you're right, the hanger is wrong

Is it almost perfect? Will a shortened hem, or small adjustment make the difference? Clothes are mass-produced, we're special. A small alteration to make a world of difference.

Men vs women

Men will go into a changeroom, find what they want, and ask when they can pick it up. Alterations are expected (garment should fit HIM). A woman will go into the changeroom, and if it doesn't fit perfectly, she'll ask what's wrong with ME

Our staff and what we like to do

Help at the changeroom

Why? There's a lot of depth and styles, we get to see it on a lot of bodies and have experience. WE can filter through and know what will look best. No work for you. It's much easier to get a new size than for you to do it

Hands-free shopping

We're happy to take you choices to the changeroom, so you're more comfortable in your search. Check size choose wisely (most women choose too big), as well we get a sense of what you like.

Your entourage

Our changerooms are large enough for your stroller, for your kids to join you. We have a safe area and a toy basket as well, if you need a brain break.

Men get their own seating area, husband parking, sofas or chairs in the back, with guy magazines to keep them entertained.

All this so you can shop stress-free and no pressure.

Chapter Sixteen: Community

Community and Advertising:

Why do you raise money for charities like the Ladies Auxiliary and Hospice?

These charities do a lot of good for our community, and we feel that it's important to support the people around us. For us, it's a pay it forward. We provide support to these charities because they help anyone in need, and at some point we all will need their services. They can provide that support to the community but they need financial support and community awareness, so when we help with a function or event we all win!

Our Theory of being Green

Reusable bags - we hire teenagers to help us behind the cash and they lovingly craft all our shopping bags by hand. We do this because our labels can then be peeled off the bags and reused (or use them SWISHed up!! We like that too) and they are recycleable as is our tissue paper and packaging. No plastic here!!

Wear it out, don't throw it out - our landfills are full of clothes and usually because they didn't work not because they're worn out. Only 23% of households will recycle their clothes or donate to a thrift store. That's a lot of waste and we'd rather you made better purchases that you love and wear for years than pieces that you discard after wearing just a few times. That's the difference between the theory of fast fashion vs slow fashion. Buy great pieces that you'll wear again and again, in great fabrics that will last and sewn with care so that they stand the test of time.

Chapter Seventeen: SWISH and why we think we're right

L istening. Our customers are great at sharing what they like and more often what they don't like about their bodies, clothes, style, shopping and we listen. We're asked all the time who the designer for SWISH is and the real answer is YOU!! You tell us what's bothering you about your body, your clothes, your shopping experience and we go off and try to fix it. We'll colour code the store because you thought it was overwhelming. It's true that we try to pack in something for everyone but if your break it down by your favourite colour then the store just got smaller, easier to manage and chances are you'll find something in your colour range quickly and easily. Fussy about a body part –arms are complained about the most!! Poor guys, they serve you well and yet we fuss about then all the time!! Solution?? Our poncho, sleevey wonder, using your scarf as a cowl shawl... the funny thing is, when it's 100 degrees out and we're really hot, all of a sudden our arms aren't so bad... cool is more important.

Making you smart

We spend lots of time with you at the change room so we can run and fetch but mostly so we can help you understand why clothes work, or don't work. When you shop in other stores and the help isn't quite so helpful it won't matter because you'll have a base knowledge for making an informed decision and therefore a wise choice. You want pieces that you love and will wear over and over. Basically we want you to wear your clothes out not throw them out no matter where you shop.

Drinks and chocolate

Shopping is and experience and entertainment. In North America it's a way to connect with girlfriends and an art form. At SWISH we think it should be the whole experience. And chocolate is just a good idea...

Conclusion

So, now you know. You know who SWISH is, what we do, and why it's important that we do. Every woman should be able to wake up in the morning, open her closet, and be able to choose something that makes her feel beautiful, confident and fabulous, effortlessly, everyday.

Clothing truly is more than just protection for our bodies, and a way to keep warm. The clothes that you choose are the first line of self-expression. This is how you show the world how you want to be seen, what you want to say, and how you're feeling, without a single word. Without the right tools, your message can get lost, and it's easy to feel misunderstood. Hopefully, we've managed to provide you with some tools to put your words in order, and step out feeling like you're your best possible self, on display for the world to adore!

In a society where women are stifled, and told that there is so much wrong with the way we look, we want to make sure you know that you are exactly right, exactly the way you are. Choosing your clothing should be a moment of empowerment, not a moment of oppression, and when you ask us to help you project the picture of who you want to show the world, we don't take that task lightly.

Join the revolution.

With Thanks

First I'd need to thank my beautiful daughter Katy whose writing talent and sassy streak brought our message to print. I wouldn't have wanted to do this project with anyone else.

Thanks to my husband Keith who has been a retail widower for the most part. Thank you for the mountain of work that you do and for keeping me on track. I am looking forward to writing our new chapter!!

To the most amazing teams!! In Gibsons, I need to thank Sophia. Wow!! What an amazing 7 years. I will always love to watch you recreate, reinvent and redesign. It has been my privilege to work alongside you.

To Mairriann, Angela, Mellissa, and Arianna, you have really been the dream team. I have looked forward to going 'to work' every day because of you. I am privileged to call you my friends.

In Castlegar, I need to thank my sister Bonnie and my mom Doreen for 'holding it all together'. Our Castlegar project has just started, how much fun to see how far we can go! Besides, retirement is overrated!!

And lastly, thank you to Angie, Jeannie, Olivia, Mackenzie, Nikki, and Shayla. For sticking it out through the 'crazy' the 'long distance' the 'what the hell does she want now?'!!! You're an amazing, talented group who have come a long way!! I look forward to taking this project for a ride!! Let's see just how far we can go!!

Ginny....

Dawn....

Dawne....

..... thank you for your friendships, for listening to me go on and on and for being the best sounding boards.

And finally, I need to thank the many women who have come through our doors, who have trusted us with their stories, their wardrobe challenges and their life changes. It's because of you that we had something to write about.

Manufactured by Amazon.ca
Bolton, ON

14535310R00057